Jordan Pinkle

My Dog Ate My Homework!

My Dog Ate My Homework!

A Collection of Funny Poems by
Bruce Lansky

Illustrated by Stephen Carpenter

**Meadowbrook Press**

Distributed by Simon & Schuster
New York

Library of Congress Cataloging-in-Publication Data

Lanksy, Bruce.
  [Poetry party]
  My dog ate my homework! : a collection of funny poems/by Bruce Lansky ;
  illustrated by Stephen Carpenter.
      p. cm.
  Originally published: Poetry party. 1996
  Includes index.
  ISBN 0-88166-406-5
  1. Children's poetry, American. 2. Humorous poetry, american. [1. American poetry.
  2. Humorous poetry.] I. Carpenter, Stephen, ill. II. Title.

  PS3562.A564 Y68 2001
  811'.54--dc21   2001031725

ISBN 0-88166-406-5
Simon & Schuster Ordering #: 0-689-02770-2

Editor: David Tobey
Graphic Designer: Linda Norton
Production: Amy Unger
Illustrator: Stephen Carpenter
Desktop Coordinator: Jay Hanson

© 1996, 2002 by Bruce Lansky

Published by Meadowbrook Press, 5451 Smetana Drive, Minnetonka, MN 55343

www.meadowbrookpress.com

BOOK TRADE DISTRIBUTION by Simon & Schuster, a division of Simon and Schuster, Inc.,
1230 Avenue of the Americas, New York, NY 10020

06 05 04 03 02   10 9 8 7 6 5 4 3 2 1

Printed in the United States of America.

Dedication

This book is dedicated to my son, Doug. When he was in elementary school, we read Shel Silverstein's *Light in the Attic* and *Where the Sidewalk Ends* together. (I recall that one of his favorite poems was "One Sister for Sale." His sister, Dana, wished there were a corresponding poem, "One Brother for Sale.")

In junior high school he chuckled over *Garfield*. In high school he enjoyed *The Far Side* and Dave Barry's books and columns. At the age of seventeen he wrote a humor book, *How to Survive High School with Minimal Brain Damage*, which sold 35,000 copies nationwide.

And now, after graduating from college and traveling around the world, he is beginning his career as a newspaper columnist—his humorous adventure travel column, "Vagabond," has been syndicated by the same company that brings us Dave Barry. Look for it in the travel section of your Sunday newspaper.

I am very proud of Doug, and I think his story is instructive. If you read to your children and encourage them to read, reading (and possibly writing) will be part of their lives.

Author's Note

When I read folk rhymes—popular poems by unknown authors, like "Roses Are Red" and "Happy Birthday to You"—I often find myself thinking of ways to vary or expand them. Here is a list of poems in this book that were inspired by folk rhymes:

My Puppy Loves Flowers; Bring Your Own Lunch; Happy Burpday to You; Jack was Nimble; Star Light, Star Bright; Our First Kiss; Scrambled; I Love You Not; Yankee Doodle's Monkey Ride; Yankee Doodle's Turtle Ride; Yankee Doodle on a Chicken; Mrs. Doodle; Say What?

Contents

Introduction viii
How to Throw a Poetry Party x
Acknowledgments xii

Parents   1

Turn Off the TV! 2
Ish! 4
My Violin 6
How to Delay Your Bedtime 8
My Prayer 10
Daddy Forgets My Name 10

Brothers and Sisters   11

My Greedy Sister 12
Bathroom Hog 13
My Noisy Brother 14
My Brother Won't Eat His Dinner 15
What My Parents Should Know about My Sister 16
What My Parents Should Know about My Brother 17
Happy Birthday from Your Loving Brother 18
My Baby Sister 19
My Sister's Always on the Phone 20

Pets   21

My Dumb Cat 22
Poorly Dressed 24
My Dog Is Too Friendly 25
My Puppy Loves Flowers 26
I'd Rather 27
Wake Up, Little Goldfish 28

School   29

A Bad Case of the Giggles 30
Most Outstanding Students of the Year Awards 32
The Teachers' Show 34
Confession 36
There's a New Cook in the Cafeteria 38
My Dog Chewed Up My Homework 40
Measles 41

New Year's Resolutions 42
Bring Your Own Lunch 44

Disasters   **45**

Someone's Toes Are in My Nose 46
Toes in My Nose 47
What's So Funny? 48
Don't Pinch! 50
Have To's 52
Oh, Woe Ith Me!. 53
What I Left Where 54
Airsick 56
Tummy Bubble 58
Rumbling in My Tummy 59
Happy Burpday to You 59
Jack Was Nimble 60
Star Light, Star Bright 61
Upset 62

All Mixed Up   **63**

Our First Kiss 64
Scrambled. 65
I Love You Not. 66
Yankee Doodle's Monkey Ride. 68
Yankee Doodle's Turtle Ride 68
Yankee Doodle on a Chicken. 69
Mrs. Doodle. 69
Clear As Mud 70
Say What?. 72

Advice   **73**

The Wrong Side of the Bed 74
Where My Clothes Are. 75
How I Quit Sucking My Thumb 76
My Thumbies 77
Manners 78
Stop Sniffling! 80

Index. 82

Introduction

I'm on a mission to get children, parents, and teachers excited about reading, writing, and performing poetry.

I learned how to write poetry for children by rewriting Mother Goose nursery rhymes to make them a lot more fun for parents to read to children and vice versa. My first poems were published in 1993 in *The New Adventures of Mother Goose*. In creating that book, I wrote new rhymes and then visited day-care centers and kindergarten classes to recite them. It was a quick way to find out whether what I'd written worked or not. That's why I wasn't surprised when *The New Adventures of Mother Goose* appeared on the *New York Times* children's poetry bestseller list.

Once I figured out how to tell a simple story in rhythm and rhyme, I visited more elementary schools to put on poetry assemblies and workshops, and to promote the anthologies I've edited: *Kids Pick the Funniest Poems* and *A Bad Case of the Giggles*. In schools, I recite my own poems, as well as those of Shel Silverstein, Jack Prelutsky, Judith Viorst, Jeffrey Moss, and others. My concept is this: If you expose children to the most entertaining children's poems ever written, they just might like poetry—reading it, performing it, and writing it.

I must say that writing poetry and sharing it with children is one of the most enjoyable things I've ever done. The response from elementary school students and teachers around the country has been overwhelming. Every time I do an assembly or workshop at a school, I am flooded with thank-you letters and poetry written by students and teachers.

In addition to all the ego gratification, I get another benefit: every time I visit a school I write more poems. I seem to do my best writing when I'm on the road to or from a school, teacher's conference, or bookstore. I'll recite a few lines of poetry out loud while I'm driving in a rented car. When I have enough material, I'll scribble down the key words at a stoplight or a gas station. I'll do my best to write down the whole poem as soon as I stop at a restaurant or at a motel for the night.

When I'm in a creative mode, everything that happens to me is material for my poetry. When I'm running late for an appointment, I think about the white rabbit in *Alice in Wonderland* and try to come up with my own poem about being late. And when I'm with children I notice these sorts of things:

- what they really think about school lunches;
- what it feels like to have a brother or sister who drives them up the wall;
- what they'd rather do instead of sitting down to finish their homework;
- the lengths they'll go to avoid eating broccoli, spinach, and liver;
- what happens when they are teased about something that's embarrassing, such as sucking their thumb or having toilet paper stuck to the bottom of their shoe after a trip to the boys or girls room;
- what it's like to have parents who tell them not to watch TV, but who watch TV themselves.

It's fun for me to take a potentially awkward or icky topic and turn it into something that makes kids laugh. That's why I think it's okay to write poems about burping and dogs who "water" the flowers. Subjects like these are part of life, have great comedic potential, and are sure to interest children who least enjoy academic studies.

When I visit schools, I try to get children excited about writing poetry as well as reading it. Writing a poem is like doing a multidimensional puzzle. There are so many things to consider: story, rhythm, rhyme, word choice, word sound, voice, mood, emotional content, metaphorical possibilities . . . the list goes on. The better students understand these elements, the better they will be at all forms of writing (and the more they will appreciate good writing).

I hope that when you read my poems you'll understand how much I enjoyed writing them and now enjoy sharing them. I also hope that you are bitten by the poetry bug that seems to have bitten me. Then you, too, will have that uncontrollable urge to share the poems you like best with the people you like best.

Bruce Lansky

How to Throw a Poetry Party

Throwing a poetry party is really quite easy, especially now that you have this book. Any book of poetry will do, but the funnier it is, the better. (Poetry about clouds or snowflakes or autumn leaves or feelings probably won't make the party as much fun.)

All you have to do is turn the next few pages of this book and start reading the poems out loud. Oh, I almost forgot to tell you that it helps if you're not all alone. Parties tend to work better when other people are around.

So you find a spot in the cafeteria, the library, your homeroom, the school bus, or wherever, and you start reading out loud. As you read, you might smile occasionally, giggle once in a while, chuckle, or even laugh out loud. Pretty soon the kids nearby (wherever you may be) become curious. They're wondering, "What's so funny?"

They start to drift closer so they can hear you read the next poem. One kid calls out, "Hey, read that one again!" Someone says, "Did you hear that one?" to his friend.

Suddenly everyone nearby is listening, watching, and laughing. The more you ham it up, the better. Now that you have everyone's attention, if you've got a fake beard, a green fright wig, or an arrow that looks like it's been shot through your head, put it on. These wacky props will hasten the moment you've been waiting for: soon someone is bound to ask, "Can I read one?"

So you reply, "What'd your mom pack for dessert?"

"Oreos."

"Got one for me?"

"Deal."

Now, everyone thinks you're clever and funny. And, you're munching on a cookie you didn't have before. That's how a poetry party starts. It's that simple.

Of course if you're in a generous mood, you can let your friends read the poems in this book without demanding an Oreo cookie. It's kind of fun to get all your friends started giggling, with or without cookies.

Well, that's all you really need to know. You can throw a poetry party almost any time. (But don't try to throw one while your teacher is delivering a boring lecture about geography or science or math. And, don't throw one with your brother or sister at bedtime. You'll probably end up fighting over this book and your parents will have to take it away. That'd be the worst thing that could happen!)

Oh, just one more thing: don't laugh too hard. You might bust a gut. (Just kidding.)

Acknowledgments

I would like to thank the following teachers and their students for helping me select the poems for this book:

Camilla Bowlin, Grassland School, Brentwood, TN; Ann Cox, Aldrich Elementary School, Omaha, NE; Sue Danielson, Withrow Elementary School, Hugo, MN; Barbara Knoss, Hanover School, Hanover, MN; Roni Graham, Central Park Elementary School, Plantation, FL; Lori Holm, Hale Elementary School, Minneapolis, MN; Julie Kaufman, Del Prado School, Boca Raton, FL; Sharon Klein, Clardy Elementary School, Kansas City, MO; Debbie Lerner, Redbridge School, Kansas City, MO; Sarah Lovelace, Groveland Elementary School, Wayzata, MN; Michelle Myer, Franklin Elementary School, Omaha, NE; Jacky Naslund, Johnsville School, Blaine, MN; Jeanne Nelson, St. Mary's Catholic School, Alexandria, MN; Elaine Nick, Gracemor Elementary School, Kansas City, MO; Tessie Oconer, Fulton School, Minneapolis, MN; Margaret Ogren, Hazeldale Elementary, Beaverton, OR; Mitzi Pearlman, Acres Green Elementary, Littleton, CO; Polly Pfeiffer, Minnetonka Intermediate School, Excelsior, MN; Barb Rannigan, Alta Vista Elementary School, Sarasota, FL; Jackie Robie, Blake Highcroft, Wayzata, MN; Melody Tenhoff, Cooper School, Hastings, MN; Vicki Wiita, Cumberland Schools, Cumberland, WI; Ron Sangalang, Sherwood Forest Elementary School, Federal Way, WA.

PARENTS

Turn Off the TV!

My father gets quite mad at me;
my mother gets upset—
when they catch me watching
our new television set.

My father yells, "Turn that thing off!"
Mom says, "It's time to study."
I'd rather watch my favorite TV show
with my best buddy.

I sneak down after homework
and turn the set on low.
But when she sees me watching it,
my mother yells out, "No!"

Dad says, "If you don't turn it off,
I'll hang it from a tree!"
I rather doubt he'll do it,
'cause he watches more than me.

He watches sports all weekend,
and weekday evenings too,
while munching chips and pretzels—
the room looks like a zoo.

So if he ever got the nerve
to hang it from a tree,
he'd spend a lot of time up there—
watching it with me.

3

Ish!

When Frederick's grandmother
served him some fish,
young Frederick turned up his nose
and said, "Ish!"

"Okay," said his grandma,
"I'll give you some ish,"
as she scraped out some earwax
right into a dish.

She brushed in some dandruff
that fell from her head,
and some fingernail clippings
from her husband, Ed.

She sniffed at the mixture
and started to sneeze.
Her eyes watered up;
she got weak in the knees.

"Okay," said Fred's grandma,
"now eat up this ish."
"No way," said young Frederick,
"I'd rather have fish."

My Violin

My mom brought home a violin
so I could learn to play.
She told me if I practiced hard
I'd play it well someday.

Without a single lesson,
I tried to play a song.
My fiddle squeaked, my fiddle squawked.
The notes came out all wrong.

My little brother fled the room.
Mom covered up her ears.
My puppy dog began to howl.
My sister was in tears.

My dad pulled out his wallet.
He handed me a ten.
He made me swear I'd never play
that violin again.

How to Delay Your Bedtime

Refuse to turn off the TV.
Say, "All my friends watch this show."

Shout, "No fair!" when you're told to go to bed.
Then ask, "Why can't I stay up till ten
like all my friends?"

When Dad says, "If all your friends
jumped off the Brooklyn Bridge,
would you jump, too?"
sneer, "Yes!"

Whine, "I'm too tired to walk upstairs to bed."
Make Dad carry you up the stairs.

Pout, "I'm too tired to brush my teeth."
Wait till Dad squeezes the toothpaste
onto your brush and starts brushing
your teeth for you.
Then groan, "Ouch, you're hurting me."

When Mom comes in to say good night
and asks you to pick up your clothes,
yawn, "I'm too tired to pick up my clothes."
Watch while Mom picks them up for you.

Beg, "I need a bedtime story."
When Mom finishes the story,
ask, "And then what happened?"

Tell her, "That story got me excited.
Now I need a backrub to make me sleepy."
When Mom starts rubbing, give directions:
"Rub a little higher.
No, a little to the left.

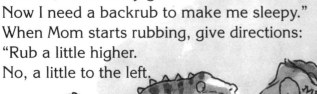

No, more to the middle."
When Mom stops rubbing,
grumble, "I was just starting to feel sleepy—
don't stop now."

When Mom says, "For the last time, good night!"
whine, "I'm thirsty.
Can I have a glass of water?"
When Mom asks you to promise
you won't wet the bed,
say, "I promise"—but cross your fingers.

Start crying.
When Dad comes to comfort you,
sob, "There's a monster under my bed."
When he turns on the lights,
you'll see it's only your shoes, socks, crayons,
and the toy you got last Christmas,
but only played with once because you lost it.
Tell him, "Leave the door open
so I can see the hall light!"
When he opens the door,
plead, "Open it wider!"

When Dad leaves,
get the toy from under your bed
and play with it in the light
shining through your doorway.

My Prayer

I pray my father finds his keys.
I pray my sister doesn't tease.
I pray that baby has no rash.
But most of all, I pray for cash.

Daddy Forgets My Name

My daddy calls me sweetie pie.
He calls me honey bunny.
He also calls me poopsie,
which I think is kind of funny.

My daddy calls me sugarplum,
and also sleepyhead.
My silly dad forgets my name
when he tucks me into bed.

BROTHERS
AND
SISTERS

My Greedy Sister

My sister's never satisfied.
She never gets enough.
She opens up her birthday gifts
and yells, "I want more stuff!"

We go out trick-or-treating
and when I start to lag,
she lightens up my load by
taking candy from my bag.

She eats dessert and screams for more,
and this I really hate,
she reaches over with her fork
and takes some from my plate.

My sister's never satisfied.
She always asks for more.
And now my very greedy sister
can't fit through the door.

Bathroom Hog

She beats me to the bathroom
and stays there for an hour.
So I can't brush my teeth because
she's singing in the shower.

She looks into the mirror
while fussing with her hair—
then throws a fit because she can't
decide what she should wear.

My sister is a bathroom hog.
I think she's very rude.
So I say, "Oink," at breakfast
when she's eating up her food.

My Noisy Brother

My brother's such a noisy kid,
when he eats soup he slurps.
When he drinks milk he gargles.
And after meals he burps.

He cracks his knuckles when he's bored.
He whistles when he walks.
He snaps his fingers when he sings,
and when he's mad he squawks.

At night my brother snores so loud
it sounds just like a riot.
Even when he sleeps
my noisy brother isn't quiet.

My Brother Won't Eat His Dinner

My brother won't eat anything
when he sits down to dinner.
Instead, he only plays with food.
Mom's worried he'll get thinner.

She offers him his favorite meal—
a burger and french fries.
My brother shuts his mouth real tight,
and then he rolls his eyes.

But I don't think that he will starve.
He likes his mother's cooking.
My sneaky brother stuffs his face
when Mother isn't looking.

What My Parents Should Know about My Sister

My sister isn't nice to me,
unless she needs a favor—
in which case for one minute
she is on her best behavior.

When she has her friends over,
she never lets me play.
She whines until my mother says
I have to go away.

I want our parents both to know
my sister makes me sore.
I hope that they will understand
I do not want one more.

What My Parents Should Know about My Brother

He wakes me in the morning.
He keeps me up at night.
He messes up my bedroom,
then starts a pillow fight.

He grabs the channel changer,
and will not give it back—
then tattles to our parents
when I give him a smack.

He blows straw wrappers at me
when we're in a restaurant.
And buys dumb birthday presents
that I would never want.

I want my parents both to know
my brother makes me sore.
I hope that they will understand
I do not want one more.

Happy Birthday from Your Loving Brother

My sister plays with Barbie dolls.
She likes to wear a skirt.
Her room's so neat and tidy that
I think she's scared of dirt.

I know I cannot change her.
But I love to see her squirm.
And so on her next birthday
I am giving her a worm.

My Baby Sister

My baby sister's
really swell.
I love her smile,
but not her smell.

My Sister's Always on the Phone

My sister's always on the phone,
I never see her study.
She doesn't do her homework,
which is why her grades are cruddy.

My sister's always on the phone,
but I don't think that's cool.
My sister is so popular
she's flunking out of school.

PETS

My Dumb Cat

My cat never comes when I call her.
She cannot remember her name.
Her brain is the size of a thimble.
And that's why my cat is so lame.

I tried to teach her to roll over,
to shake, beg, and fetch wooden sticks.
We practiced and practiced and practiced.
My dumb cat could not learn the tricks.

Then one day my cat was a hero.
She captured a small, squeaky mouse.
She hid the dead mouse in the sofa.
My dumb cat stunk up the whole house.

I wonder why cats were invented.
They eat and they drink and they purr.
There's only one trick they know how to do:
they sit on your lap and shed fur.

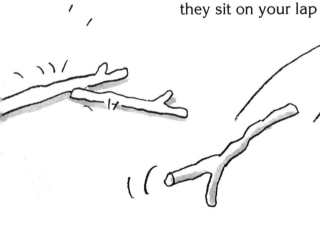

Poorly Dressed

I have a friend who's not well dressed.
He wears no hat. He wears no vest.

Upon his back he wears no shirt,
so you can see there's lots of dirt.

He wears no shoes upon his feet.
He wears no pants upon his seat.

In fact, he doesn't wear a stitch,
so he can scratch if there's an itch.

I hope that you don't find him rude—
my dog is happy in the nude.

My Dog Is Too Friendly

My dog is very friendly,
but he sometimes gets excited—
especially when we've been apart
and then are reunited.

He puts his paws up on my waist,
then barks and gives a push.
I tumble over backwards
and I land right on my tush.

My dog feels very sorry
and he licks me without fail.
He licks my ears and cheeks and nose,
then wags his little tail.

I hate it when he licks me,
but I do not have much hope.
His breath smells like a garbage dump.
He should be using Scope.

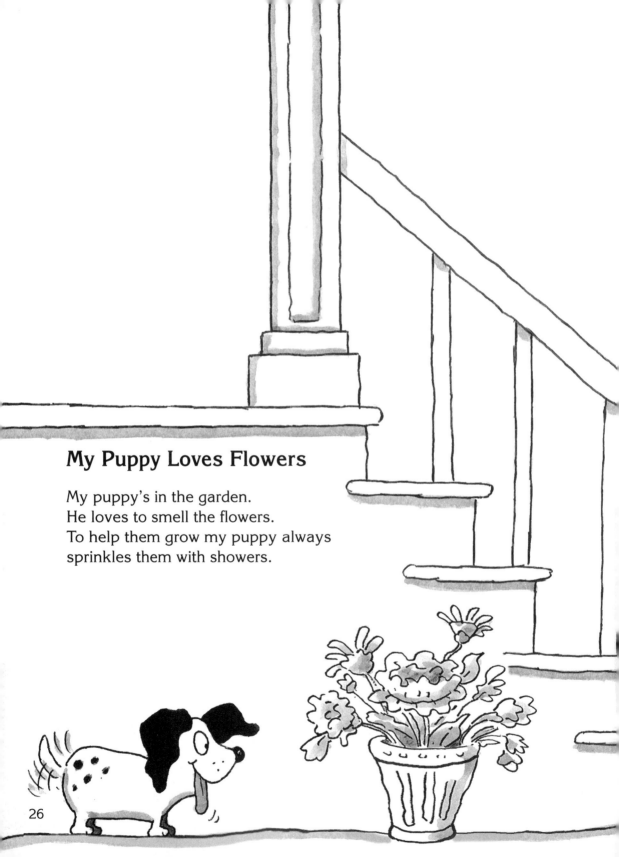

My Puppy Loves Flowers

My puppy's in the garden.
He loves to smell the flowers.
To help them grow my puppy always
sprinkles them with showers.

26

I'd Rather

I'd rather wash the dishes.
I'd rather kiss a frog.
I'd rather get an F in math
or run a ten-mile jog.

I'd rather do my homework.
I'd rather mow the lawn.
I'd rather take the garbage out.
I'd rather wake at dawn.

I'd rather dine on Brussels sprouts
or catch the chicken pox.
I'd rather do most anything
than clean the litter box.

Wake Up, Little Goldfish

Why do you float for days on end
and stay so very still?
I wonder if you're sleeping.
I wonder if you're ill.

I wish you'd move around a bit—
swim to the top, then dive.
I wish you'd eat your goldfish food,
so I'd know that you're alive.

SCHOOL

A Bad Case of the Giggles

I found a book of poems.
I brought the book to school.
And every time I read it
I giggle like a fool.

Today in social studies
I opened up the book.
I started giggling right away
just from a single look.

I'm croaking like a bullfrog.
I'm braying like a mule.
These aren't sounds you're supposed to make
while studying at school.

The more I try to stop it
the louder that I howl.
I'm squawking like a parrot,
and hooting like an owl!

I'm making a commotion;
the teacher is upset.
I'm losing my position
as teacher's favorite pet!

My giggling is contagious.
My friends have all joined in.
The teacher's getting angry.
We're making quite a din.

The whole darned class is giggling.
Not one of us can stop.
The teacher says that if we can't
he'll call the hallway cop.
The room next door has heard us.
And now they're giggling too.
The sound of giggling travels fast.
The school sounds like a zoo.

And now the teacher's giving up.
He cannot teach today.
The principal's declaring it
a giggling holiday.

Most Outstanding Students of the Year Awards*

I'm making this announcement
to honor_____best.
            [school's name]
I think that you will all agree
they rose above the rest.

Our most outstanding artist
is Christopher McKnight.
He's the one who painted all the
classroom blackboards white.

Our most outstanding sportsman
is Stephen Montague.
He scored a basket for his team—
and the opponents', too.

  * *Fill in the blanks with the
    name of your school.*

The student teachers like the best
is Alexander Brash.
Most kids give teachers apples.
But Alex gave them cash.

The winner for attendance
is Mary Anne McKay.
She came to school on every day
of Christmas holiday.

Congratulations, winners!
Let's all give them a cheer—
the_____Elementary
              [school's name]
students of the year.

The Teachers' Show*

I have an important announcement.
I want everybody to know:
on Monday all classes are cancelled.
The teachers will put on a show.

_____ will be juggling meatballs.
[Teacher's name]

_____ will dance with a bear.
[Teacher's name]

_____ and _____ will yodel.
[Teacher's name]   [Teacher's name]

_____ will tear out _____ hair.
[Teacher's name]   [his or her]

_____ is quite entertaining.
[Teacher's name]

_____ does something you've never seen.
[He or She]

If you want a bad case of measles,
_____ paint them on red, white, and green.
[He'll or She'll]

_____ is also performing.
[Principal's name]

_____ come up with something quite new.
[He's or She's]

_____ doing _____ act in the kitchen.
[He's or She's]   [his or her]

_____ dumping the cook in the stew.
[He's or She's]

Your parents are certainly welcome,
but make sure to tell them the rule.
If any of them arrive tardy,
they'll have to be kept after school.

I know that our show is exciting.
I wish that you all could be here.
But school will be closed for vacation.
I can't wait to see you next year.

Fill in the blanks with the names of teachers in your school.

34

Confession

I have a brief confession
that I would like to make.
If I don't get it off my chest
I'm sure my heart will break.

I didn't do my reading.
I watched TV instead—
while munching cookies, cakes, and chips
and cinnamon raisin bread.

I didn't wash the dishes.
I didn't clean the mess.
Now there are roaches eating crumbs—
a million, more or less.

I didn't turn the TV off.
I didn't shut the light.
Just think of all the energy
I wasted through the night.

I feel so very guilty.
I did a lousy job.
I hope my students don't find out
that I am such a slob.

There's a New Cook in the Cafeteria

Good morning, staff and students.
We have a brand new cook.
And that's why our lunch menu
will have a brand new look.

To make a good impression,
our cook's prepared a treat:
your choice of snapping turtle soup
or deep-fried monkey meat.

If you're a vegetarian
we have good news today:
she's serving pickled cauliflower
and jellyfish soufflé.

And for dessert our cook has made
a recipe from France:
I'm sure you'll all want seconds—
of chocolate-covered ants.

I hope you like this gourmet feast.
I hope you won't complain.
But if you do we'll have to bring
our old cook back again.

My Dog Chewed Up My Homework

I'm glad to say my homework's done.
I finished it last night.
I've got it right here in this box.
It's not a pretty sight.

My dog chewed up my homework.
He slobbered on it, too.
So now my homework's ripped to shreds
and full of slimy goo.

It isn't much to look at,
but I brought it anyway.
I'm going to dump it on your desk
if I don't get an A.

Measles

There are measles on my forehead.
There are measles on my nose.
There are measles on my elbows.
There are measles on my toes.

There are measles on the carpet.
There are measles on the chair.
There are measles on my glasses
There are measles in my hair.

I'm so tired of painting measles.
I would like to take a rest.
I sure hope I have enough to be
excused from tomorrow's test.

New Year's Resolutions

Last year I did some rotten things.
This year I will be better.
Here are some resolutions
I will follow to the letter:

I won't make dumb excuses
when my homework isn't done;
when the truth is that I did no work
'cause I was having fun.

I won't fly paper airplanes
when the teacher isn't looking.
I won't sneak in the kitchen
just to taste what they are cooking.

I will not twist the silverware
to see how far it bends.
I will not take the candy bars
from lunch bags of my friends.

I will not skateboard down the hall
or skateboard down the stairs.
I won't run over teachers,
and I won't crash into chairs.

I will not do these rotten things;
my heart is full of sorrow.
But I have got some brand-new tricks
to try in school tomorrow.

Bring Your Own Lunch

Don't eat school lunches—
not even a lick.
They might make you nauseous.
They might make you sick.

Just take a small bite and
you'll start to feel ill.
If the veggies don't get you,
the meatloaf sure will.

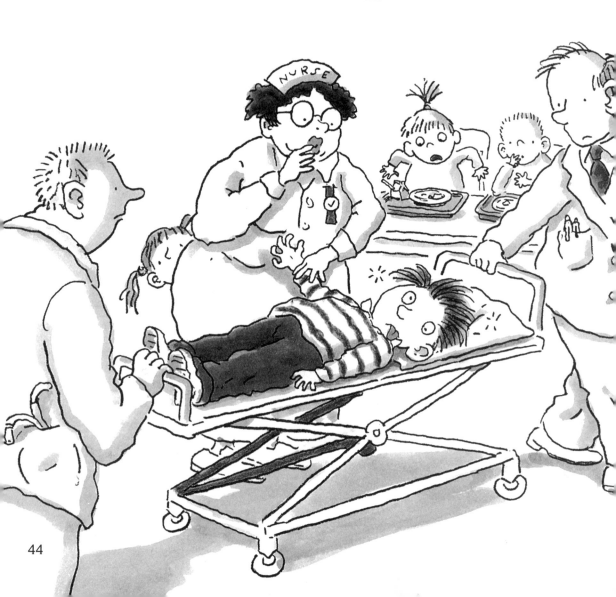

DISASTERS

Someone's Toes Are in My Nose

Someone's toes are in my nose.
Whosever could they be?
Since no one else is in my bed,
they must belong to me!

I wonder how it happened.
I just don't understand.
I don't know how my legs got stretched
out like a rubber band.

How will I ever get to school?
It's a catastrophe!
Mother! Dad! Get on the phone
and dial some help for me!

Please call the fire department.
Tell them to send a truck.
And have a 'copter standing by
in case the truck gets stuck.

Then call the plastic surgeon.
We'll need one—just in case.
I do not want a single scratch
or blemish on my face.

My problem's so ridiculous,
I think I'm going mad.
If not, this is the weirdest dream
that I have ever had.

Toes in My Nose

I bet that I could do it.
My friends all said, "No way."
And now my toes are in my nose,
so they will have to pay.

They each owe me a dollar—
of that there is no doubt.
There's just one little problem.
I cannot get them out.

What's So Funny?

There's something no one's telling me.
There's something I don't know.
I notice people staring at me
everywhere I go.

I ask my friends to clue me in;
not knowing is distressing.
But no one says a single word;
I find that quite depressing.

They point at me and giggle.
They point at me and grin.
I'll have to find out just what kind
of trouble I am in.

I check the bathroom mirror
to learn the awful truth.
I find a piece of lettuce
sticking on my big front tooth.

I rinse the yucky green away.
I think that is the end.
But then I hear more giggling—
it comes from my best friend.

I tell him, "Jack, please help me out,
I'm feeling kind of blue."
He says, "You've got some toilet paper
sticking to your shoe!"

Don't Pinch!

When I got on the school bus,
I was in for a surprise.
My friends all stared and pointed.
There was mischief in their eyes.

A kid who sat in front of me
reached out and pinched my knee.
My friends all started laughing,
but the joke was lost on me.

And then I got a second pinch.
I felt it on my ear.
And then I felt a third and fourth.
You guessed it—on my rear.

I asked, "Why are you pinching me?
I think it's very mean!"
They said, "Today's St. Patrick's Day
and you're not wearing green."

Have To's

I have to catch the bus to school,
where I must stay till three.
There are a lot of places that
I'd really rather be.

Then after school I have to practice
piano every day.
I have to do my homework, too,
before Mom lets me play.

At suppertime I have to wash
my hands and feed my fishes.
And after supper I must clear
my place and wash the dishes.

At night I have to brush and floss—
that's what my dentist said.
And when the clock says nine o'clock,
I have to go to bed.

I have to end this poem now.
I have to—I can't wait.
I have to find the bathroom soon,
before it is too late.

Oh, Woe Ith Me!

Ath I wath biking
down the thtweet,
I hit a bump
and lotht my theat.

I cwathed my bike
into a twee.
I thcwathed my fathe—
oh, woe ith me.

My bike ith wecked.
I've no excuthe.
And wortht of all,
my tooth ith looth.

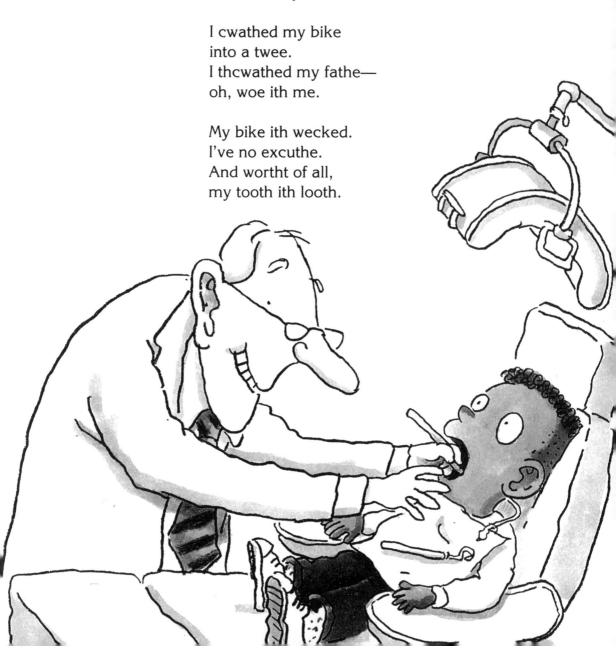

What I Left Where

I left my lunch bag on the bus;
the lunchroom teachers made a fuss.

I left my glasses in the car;
without them I cannot go far.

I left my mittens in the snow;
that's not where they're supposed to go.

I left my schoolbooks back at school.
I left my swimsuit at the pool.

I left my bike out in the rain.
I left my suitcase on a plane.

And, since my memory's not too great,
I left my spinach on my plate.

Airsick

My first time flying in a plane
was an experience.
I would have traveled in a bus
if I had had more sense.

The pilot said, "Now buckle up.
We'll soon be in the air."
I held my breath, I gripped my seat,
I said a little prayer.

And then when we had taken off
I tried to read a book.
I started feeling sleepy—
just from a single look.

I put the book down on my seat
and closed my eyes to nap.
A steward serving coffee poured
some right into my lap.

The bathrooms were all occupied
just when I had to go.
I crossed my legs and squeezed them tight—
the bathroom line was slow.

A stewardess was passing by.
She told me I looked sick.
She handed me an airsick pill
she hoped would do the trick.

She handed me a barfing bag
to use if I felt queasy.
I wonder why I ever thought
that flying would be easy.

Tummy Bubble

A burp is just a bubble
that forms inside your tum.
But if it goes the other way,
say nothing, just play dumb.

Happy Burpday to You

Happy burpday to you.
You belong in the zoo.
When you burp say excuse me.
That's the right thing to do.

Rumbling in My Tummy

I can't stop my tummy from rumbling.
I shouldn't have eaten so fast.
Tomorrow I'll eat much more slowly,
so I won't be filled up with gas.

Jack Was Nimble

Jack was nimble.
Jack was quick.
Jack jumped over
the candlestick.

Jack kept jumping
much too close.
Now his pants
smell like burnt toast.

60

Star Light, Star Bright

Star light, star bright,
first star I see tonight,
I'm going to try with all my might
to keep my jammies dry all night.

Upset

Nothing makes me
quite upset
as waking in a
bed that's wet.

ALL MIXED UP

Our First Kiss

How well I remember
the first time we kissed.
We both closed our eyes,
then we puckered and missed.

Scrambled

I climbed up the door and
I opened the stairs.
I said my pajamas
and buttoned my prayers.

I turned off the covers
and pulled up the light.
I'm all scrambled up since
she kissed me last night.

I Love You Not

I love you I love you,
I love you so well,
if I had a skunk
I would give you a smell.

If I were a dog
I would give you a bite.
If I were a witch
I would give you a fright.

If I were a bathtub
I'd give you a splash.
If I were a fungus
I'd give you a rash.

I love you so much
that I won't tell a lie,
I promise we'll marry
the day that I die.

Yankee Doodle's Monkey Ride

Yankee Doodle went to town
riding on a monkey.
He had to take a shower quick
because he smelled so funky.

Yankee Doodle's Turtle Ride

Yankee Doodle went to town
riding on a turtle.
His belly jiggled all around,
so now he wears a girdle.

Yankee Doodle on a Chicken

Yankee Doodle went to town
riding on a chicken.
He went into a restaurant
and came out finger lickin'.

Mrs. Doodle

Mrs. Doodle went to town
riding on a gator.
She didn't feed the gator,
so the hungry gator ate 'er.

Clear As Mud

I go to bed each morning.
I wake up every night.
I spill my milk at breakfast,
and then turn on the light.

Each day I miss the school bus.
I never have been late.
I don't turn in my homework.
My teacher thinks I'm great.

My favorite game is basketball.
I cannot sink a shot.
We haven't won a single game.
Our team is getting hot!

Last year I was in high school.
Now I'm in second grade.
Next year I'll be in daycare.
I'll really have it made!

When I grow up, I'm hoping
a baby I can be:
a pacifier in my mouth,
my cradle in a tree.

This poem's so confusing.
It's all so crystal clear.
Perhaps I'll understand it
when I am born next year.

Say What?

One fine October morning
in April, last July,
the moon fell on my window,
the rain shone in the sky.

The flowers sang quite sweetly.
The birds were in full bloom.
I dumped the neighbors' garbage
inside our dining room.

My parents always praise me
for sneaking out of school.
They tell me not to study,
so I won't be a fool.

My favorite food is spinach.
It makes my muscles small.
Each day I'm growing shorter—
soon I'll be eight feet tall!

I'm saving up my money
to throw it all away.
I hope this poem annoys you,
so have a happy day.

ADVICE

The Wrong Side of the Bed

I'm looking in the mirror.
I don't like what I see.
My eyes look tired and bloodshot.
This isn't really me.

My socks are different colors.
My shirt is not tucked in.
My hair looks like a hurricane
from Cuba just blew in.

I'm feeling very grumpy.
I'm in a rotten mood.
I snapped at breakfast when Mom said
to get my own darned food.

When I get in a cranky state,
I wish that I could hide.
Mom says, "Go back to bed and
get up on the other side."

Where My Clothes Are

Dirty clothes should be put in the hamper.
Clean clothes should be put in the drawer.
But it takes too much time and it takes too much work,
so I throw them all over the floor.

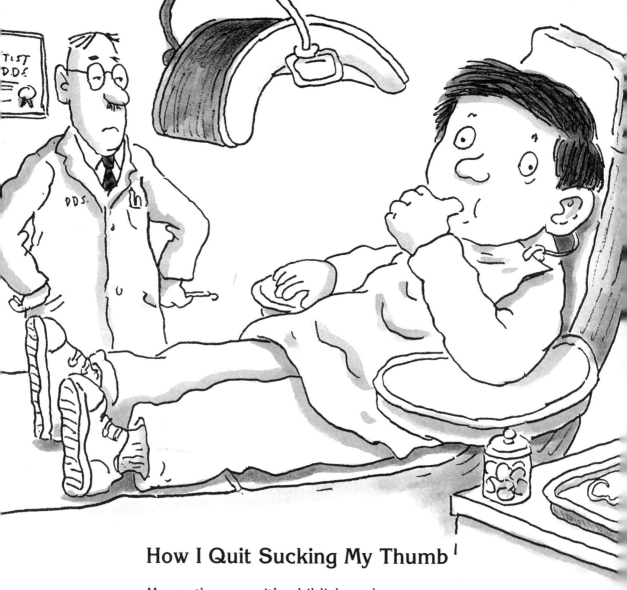

How I Quit Sucking My Thumb

My mother says it's childish and
my father says it's dumb—
whenever they discover that
I'm sucking on my thumb.

It's such a silly thing to do,
as everybody knows.
So now instead of sucking it
I stick it in my nose.

My Thumbies

I have two little thumbies.
They're with me day and night.
My favorite thumb is on my left.
The other's on my right.

My thumbies always comfort me
when I am feeling sad.
They help me to protect myself
when I am feeling mad.

My thumbies help me fall asleep
when I am feeling tired.
I do not know how better friends
could ever be desired.

My mother says it's time to quit—
that sucking thumbs is bad.
And every time I suck my thumb,
my mom gets very mad.

"You've got to quit. Don't suck your thumbs—
your left one or your right.
It's pushing all your front teeth out.
It's ruining your bite.

"It might take years to get straight teeth,
with braces on your mouth.
It isn't fun. Believe me, son.
So keep your thumbs down south."

I'm forty-nine. It's time to quit—
of all the silly habits.
I don't want people thinking that
my teeth look like a rabbit's.

Manners

Manners are useless.
Take my advice.
Always act rudely.
Never be nice.

Eat with your fingers,
not with a fork.
Don't use a napkin.
Why be a dork?

Don't change your clothing.
Dress like a bum.
Don't do your homework.
Try to act dumb.

Never say, "Thank you."
Never say, "Please."
Don't say, "I'm sorry."
It's better to tease.

If you remember
to do what I say,
you'll have no more friends
when you call them to play.

Stop Sniffling!

If you should have the sniffles,
you'd better blow your nose.
Because if you should go "Achoo!"
you'll mess up all your clothes.

Index

Airsick, 56

Bad Case of the Giggles, A, 30
Bathroom Hog, 13
Bring Your Own Lunch, 44

Clear As Mud, 70
Confession, 36

Daddy Forgets My Name, 10
Don't Pinch!, 50

Happy Birthday from Your Loving Brother, 18
Happy Burpday to You, 59
Have To's, 52
How I Quit Sucking My Thumb, 76
How to Delay Your Bedtime, 8

I Love You Not, 66
I'd Rather, 27
Ish!, 4

Jack Was Nimble, 60

Manners, 78
Measles, 41
Most Outstanding Students of the Year Award, 32
Mrs. Doodle, 69
My Baby Sister, 19
My Brother Won't Eat His Dinner, 15
My Dog Chewed Up My Homework, 40
My Dog Is Too Friendly, 25
My Dumb Cat, 22
My Greedy Sister, 12
My Noisy Brother, 14

My Prayer, 10
My Puppy Loves Flowers, 26
My Sister's Always on the Phone, 20
My Thumbies, 77
My Violin, 6

New Year's Resolutions, 42

Oh, Woe Ith Me!, 53
Our First Kiss, 64

Poorly Dressed, 24

Rumbling in My Tummy, 59

Say What?, 72
Scrambled, 65
Someone's Toes Are in My Nose, 46
Star Light, Star Bright, 61
Stop Sniffling!, 80

Teacher's Show, The, 34
There's a New Cook in the Cafeteria, 38
Toes in My Nose, 47
Tummy Bubble, 58
Turn Off the TV!, 2

Upset, 62

Wake Up, Little Goldfish, 28
What I Left Where, 54
What My Parents Should Know about My Brother, 17
What My Parents Should Know about My Sister, 16
What's So Funny?, 48
Where My Clothes Are, 75
Wrong Side of the Bed, The, 74

Yankee Doodle on a Chicken, 69
Yankee Doodle's Monkey Ride, 68
Yankee Doodle's Turtle Ride, 68

What People Say about Bruce Lansky's Poetry:

What librarians say:

"Bruce Lansky's poetry books are so funny, we can't keep them on our library shelves."
—Lynette Townsend, Lomarena Elementary, Laguna Hills, California

"As soon as the library opens in the morning, there is a line of children waiting for Bruce Lansky's poetry books."
—Kay Winek, Pattison Elementary, Superior, Wisconsin

What teachers say:

"Some of my students don't like reading, but once they open one of Lansky's poetry books, I can't get them to close it."
—Suzanna Thompson, Holy Name Elementary, Wayzata, MN

"Bruce Lansky turns reluctant readers into avid readers."—Sharon Klein, Clardy Elementary, Kansas City, MO

"Bruce Lansky is the 'Pied Piper of Poetry.' He gets children excited about reading and writing poetry."—Mary Wong, Explorer Middle School, Phoenix, AZ

"There's no doubt about it—Bruce Lansky is the king of giggle poetry."—Jody Bolla, North Miami Elementary, Aventura, FL

What critics say:

"Guaranteed to elicit laughs when read alone or aloud to a class."—*Booklist*

"When I read any of his poems, it's giggles galore."—*Instructor* magazine

What kids say about Bruce Lansky's gigglepoetry.com:

"I really like your site. I used to hate poetry, but you guys make it fun."—Christina, Texas

"Even though I'm from outer space, I can speak and read your language. These poems are cool. On my planet, all we ever do is sit around and watch TV."
—Me, Outer Space

"I really love this website. It is awesome! It gives me stuff to do when I am grounded."
—Tiffany, Enid, Oklahoma

"I think these poems are the best poems ever!!! If you ever get down, they will make you feel better!!! —Hadassah, Augusta, Georgia

"My teacher wanted to read some poems. I gave her some I found on gigglepoetry.com. The whole class laughed like mad zombies."
—Jolin, Singapore

Poetry Books by Bruce Lansky:

A Bad Case of the Giggles
Kids Pick the Funniest Poems
Miles of Smiles
Poetry Party

Happy Birthday to Me!
The New Adventures of Mother Goose
No More Homework! No More Tests!
Sweet Dreams

For information about inviting poet/author Bruce Lansky to your school or conference, or to order a free Meadowbrook Press catalog, write or call toll free:

Meadowbrook Press, 5451 Smetana Drive, Minnetonka, MN 55343, 800-338-2232
www.meadowbrookpress.com   www.gigglepoetry.com